# Technology TITANS

# Larry Page, Sergey Brin, and Google

Hal Marcovitz

ReferencePoint Press®

San Diego, CA

© 2016 ReferencePoint Press, Inc.
Printed in the United States

**For more information, contact:**
ReferencePoint Press, Inc.
PO Box 27779
San Diego, CA 92198
www.ReferencePointPress.com

LIBRARY OF CONGRESS CATALOGING-IN-PUBLICATION DATA

Marcovitz, Hal.
  Larry Page, Sergey Brin, and Google / by Hal Marcovitz.
    pages cm. -- (Technology titans)
  Audience: Grade 9 to 12.
  Includes bibliographical references and index.
  ISBN-13: 978-1-60152-874-2 (hardback)
  ISBN-10: 1-60152-874-4 (hardback)
  1. Page, Larry, 1973- 2. Brin, Sergey, 1973- 3. Computer programmers--United States--Biography--Juvenile literature. 4. Telecommunications engineers--United States--Biography--Juvenile literature. 5. Webmasters--United States--Biography--Juvenile literature. 6. Businesspeople--United States--Biography--Juvenile literature. 7. Google--Juvenile literature. 8. Google (Firm)--Juvenile literature. I. Title.
  QA76.2.A2M366 2015
  005.1--dc23
                                                                    2015012258

# Contents

# Managing the World's Information

In 2006 the editors of the *Merriam-Webster's Collegiate Dictionary* announced their decision to include the word *google* in the following year's edition of the online dictionary. The word was included as a verb, and the dictionary defined it as: "To use the Google search engine to obtain information about (as a person) on the World Wide Web."[1] In other words, according to the *Merriam-Webster* editors, if somebody desires to look up the capital of North Dakota on the Internet, they would google "North Dakota" and "state capital" and within no more than a second or so be rewarded with the answer: Bismarck. Or if a researcher desired to know the winner of the 1994 Academy Award for Best Picture, googling the keywords "Oscar," "1994" and "Best Picture" would reveal the answer: *Forrest Gump*.

The actual proper noun, *Google*, is not included in the dictionary. Google is, in fact, a copyrighted name—it is not only the name of the popular search engine but also the name of the huge American corporation that developed and owns the search engine. Still, the fact that the dictionary decided to accept *google* as a legitimate word in the English language suggests the two young computer engineers who developed the Google search engine—Sergey Brin and Larry Page—have created more than a tool for computer users; they have shaped an element of global culture.

Each day about 1.2 billion people conduct Google searches—that is about 17 percent of the world's population. Google users initiate 40,000 searches per second or roughly 1.2 trillion searches per year. That is a lot of googling.

## Google's Mission Statement

In 1996, when Page and Brin began writing the computer program that eventually turned into Google, they never envisioned that the search engine would one day dominate the World Wide Web. They were simply two computer science students exploring a problem they found fascinating: how to find and organize information on the Internet. Says Page:

> We were doing research at Stanford University. Google sort of came out of that. And we didn't even intend to build a search engine originally. We were just interested in the Web and interested in data mining. And then we ended up with search technology that we realized was really good. And we built the search engine. Then we told our friends about it and our professors. Pretty soon, about 10,000 people a day were using it.[2]

Eventually, though, the pair saw the value in making Google into a commercial venture. And soon after establishing their company in 1998, Brin and Page wrote a mission statement—a declaration of the purpose of Google, one that all employees are expected to follow. Google's mission statement reads: "To organize the world's information and make it universally accessible and useful."[3]

> "We didn't even intend to build a search engine originally. We were just interested in the Web and interested in data mining."[2]
>
> —Google cocreator Larry Page.

## Explosive Growth

When Page and Brin wrote that mission statement, the Internet was far smaller than it is today. In 1998 there were some 2 million websites available on the Internet. Today there are more than 1 billion. And yet Google has managed to keep up with the explosive growth of the Internet, meaning that the mission statement written by the founders two decades ago remains the company's purpose today. Brin says:

> Our mission is to make the world's information accessible and useful. And that means all of the world's information. . . . In history,

you have never had access to just pretty much all of the world's information in seconds, and we have that now, and to make it really useful, you have to have a way of finding whatever it is that you want. That's precisely what we work on at Google. My hope is to provide instant access to any information anybody ever wants in the future.[4]

Larry Page (left) and Sergey Brin (right) had a specific purpose in mind for their new company when they established it in 1998. The company's mission remains essentially the same today: to organize all of the world's information and make it accessible and useful.

## Affecting Billions of Lives

The original mission statement written by Brin and Page may remain the guiding philosophy for Google, but in the two decades since the two entrepreneurs founded the company, they have also taken Google in new directions, making it much more than an organization that manages a search engine. Indeed, Google has emerged as a leader in many facets of Internet culture, providing entertainment through Google Play, directions for travelers through Google Maps, and views of the planet through Google Earth—to cite a few of the company's many projects. Each day millions of people access videos on YouTube, which is owned by Google, making YouTube one of the Internet's premier sites for entertainment.

"In history, you have never had access to just pretty much all of the world's information in seconds, and [with Google] we have that now."[4]

—Google cocreator Sergey Brin.

These endeavors have helped make Google into one of the largest companies in America. Google's value in early 2015 was estimated at $371 billion, making it the fourth-largest corporation in the country. (The three larger companies are computer and smartphone maker Apple, oil giant ExxonMobil, and software developer Microsoft.)

Clearly, Google has evolved since its earliest days as an organization dedicated to managing the world's information and making it accessible. And in overseeing Google's evolution, Brin and Page find themselves leading one of the world's most innovative companies—an organization that affects the lives of billions of people worldwide.

# Chapter 1

# Brin and Page: Their Paths to Stanford

Sergey Brin and Larry Page were both born in 1973. They grew up in similar households—their parents were employed in fields that called on their skills as mathematicians and scientists. As young people, Brin and Page also excelled in math and the sciences and were drawn to careers in the emerging field of computer science. They finally met at Stanford University in 1995. But their paths to Stanford could not have been more different, and in fact, their journeys to the university in Northern California started nearly 6,000 miles (9,656 km) apart.

## Brin: A Jew in the Soviet Union

Sergey Brin was born in the former Soviet Union, the son of Michael and Eugenia Brin. Sergey grew up in an environment where math and science were part of everyday life. Michael studied mathematics at Moscow State University; Eugenia was a civil engineer employed by the Soviet Oil and Gas Institute. In America, scientists and engineers of the caliber of the Brins were in much demand by major corporations and top universities. There the Brins would likely have commanded top salaries and been able to afford a fine home, expensive automobiles, and all the other luxuries available to people of their intelligence and accomplishments. But as citizens of the former Soviet Union, they lived in no more than modest circumstances. Moreover, the Brins are Jews, and therefore, they suffered under the institutionalized anti-Semitism of the Soviet state.

Sergey's father, for example, aspired to study astrophysics. But since physics and nuclear science shared the same department at the university, he was barred from entering the department because authorities did not trust Jews with access to knowledge about nuclear physics, fearing they would leak the Soviet Union's weapons science to the United States. This was the era of the Cold War, when the Soviet Union and United States were highly suspicious of each other. Both nations were involved in long-standing weapons development projects as deterrents against nuclear strikes by the other side. That was the tense Soviet climate in which the Brins were forced to live.

## Escape Before the Collapse

Michael left Moscow State University with a PhD in mathematics; despite his advanced degree, as a Jew in the Soviet Union his opportunities were limited. Eugenia also faced discrimination at her workplace and was barred from advancement. As such, the Brins lived in a small apartment in Moscow, which they shared with Sergey's grandmother, a teacher. Recalls Sergey, "We were quite poor. My parents, both of them, went through periods of hardship."[5]

> "We were quite poor. My parents, both of them, went through periods of hardship."[5]
>
> —Google cocreator Sergey Brin.

Michael Brin managed to find a job as an economist with Gosudarstvennyy Planovyy Komitet—in English, the State Planning Committee. Known more familiarly as Gosplan, the agency was charged with advising the Soviet Union's Communist regime on economic policy. Essentially, Gosplan advised officials on which segments of Soviet industry, agriculture, and business should be supported by the government. However, by the time Brin arrived at Gosplan in 1969, the Soviet Union's economy had already started on a path toward collapse that would end in 1991 when the huge country split apart. During the decade Brin worked at Gosplan, it was his job to study statistics of the Soviet Union's dismal industrial output and alter them so they appeared to support the notion that a Communist regime—in which the government manages all industry—is far superior to the American system, which is based on private enterprise. "Much of the time I devoted to proving that Russian living standards were much, much higher than the American living standards,"[6] he says.

Sergey Brin's early years were spent in Moscow, the home of Saint Basil's Cathedral (pictured), the Kremlin, and Red Square. As Jews in the former Soviet Union, the Brin family had limited opportunities. Eventually they obtained permission to immigrate to the United States.

In 1977 Brin attended an international conference of economists in Warsaw, Poland. He already knew that the Soviet Union's economy was heading for collapse and that his family, as Jews, would have limited opportunities in Moscow. His discussions with other economists convinced him that many opportunities were available to mathematicians in the West. When he arrived home from Poland, Brin announced to his family, "We cannot stay here anymore. We have to leave."[7]

# Refuseniks

Brin applied for permission to leave the USSR and immigrate to the United States. The Brins were denied permission, thus becoming refuseniks—the term applied to Jews denied permission to leave the Soviet Union. Moreover, as refuseniks, the Brins found themselves the victims of even harsher treatment by the Soviet government. Michael was fired from Gosplan. Eugenia was also advised to quit her job. After living in near poverty for the next two years, the Brins were finally granted permission to leave the USSR. They left in May 1979.

Just five years old, Sergey traveled with his family first to Vienna, Austria, then to Paris, France, where his father took a brief job as they made plans to find a home in America. They were aided by the Hebrew Immigrant Aid Society, which helped former refuseniks find new homes and jobs. Finally, on October 25, 1979, the Brins boarded a flight to America, arriving at John F. Kennedy International Airport in New York City.

Little Sergey recalled his first images of America: Sitting in the backseat of a car driven by a family friend from Moscow, he watched as traffic zipped by on the Long Island Expressway. Sergey had never seen so many cars in his life.

> "Much of the time I devoted to proving that Russian living standards were much, much higher than the American living standards."[6]
>
> —Michael Brin, father of Sergey Brin.

Michael soon found a job as a mathematics professor at the University of Maryland in College Park, about 8 miles (13 km) north of Washington, DC. The Brins' first home was a modest cinderblock house in a working-class neighborhood near Baltimore. "My parents sort of lived in the dining room," Sergey recalls. "There was no wall between the dining room and the kitchen. They used that as their bedroom."[8] The home was still far superior to the cramped apartment they shared in Moscow. But their home life soon improved, especially after Eugenia found a position as an engineer at the National Aeronautics and Space Administration (NASA) Goddard Space Flight Center in nearby Greenbelt, Maryland.

# Math Prodigy

Sergey had been born into a family of mathematicians and scientists—his grandfather had also been a math professor and his great-grandmother a biologist. As Sergey grew older, his talents in math and science emerged as well. When he turned nine years old, his parents gave him a Commodore 64—one of the first computers manufactured for consumer use. Soon after receiving the computer, he wrote his first software program—a computer game he made up that featured warring armies.

He also inherited his family's prowess in mathematics. On one occasion, the child listened as his father discussed a math problem with a

## Sergey Brin's Return to the Soviet Union

In 1990, a year before the Soviet Union collapsed and split into fifteen separate countries, sixteen-year-old Sergey Brin returned to Moscow. He accompanied his father, Michael, who led a group of high school students on a visit to what was then the Russian Soviet Socialist Republic, a state within the Communist nation. When Sergey left the Soviet Union, he was just five years old, and therefore he remembered little of his former homeland. But he had heard his parents talk about their dismal life in Moscow, especially after they became refuseniks. As he surveyed the crumbling city and its unhappy residents, he knew how limited his opportunities would have been had the Brins elected to stay in Russia. On his second day in Moscow, he took his father aside and said, "Thank you for taking us all out of Russia."

Later in the trip Sergey's rebelliousness emerged. Angered at the totalitarianism of the Soviet state, Brin hurled pebbles at a Moscow police car. The car stopped. Two police officers emerged and were livid at the boy's mischief, but Michael Brin was able to defuse their anger when he promised Sergey would be disciplined. Says Sergey, "My rebelliousness, I think, came out of being born in Moscow. . . . I'd say this is something that followed me into adulthood."

Quoted in Mark Malseed, "The Story of Sergey Brin," *Moment*, February–March 2007. www.momentmag .com/the-story-of-sergey-brin.

teaching colleague—it was a problem Michael's university students had failed to solve. During the conversation, Sergey interrupted his father and suggested an answer. At first, Michael ignored his son, but Michael's startled colleague pointed out to his friend that the boy had just solved the problem.

The Brins enrolled Sergey in the Paint Branch Montessori School in Adelphi, Maryland. Schools that teach through the Montessori method—founded by Italian educator Maria Montessori—do not operate as traditional schools, with students seated in classrooms and taking notes as teachers guide them through lessons. Instead, Montessori students are granted widespread freedom to study what interests them most and spend as much time on a topic as they desire. Students are also encouraged to solve problems on their own.

At first, Sergey struggled at Paint Branch—he was still learning to speak English and, moreover, was naturally shy and withdrawn. "It was a difficult year for him, the first year," recalls Eugenia. "We were constantly discussing the fact we had been told that children are like sponges, that they immediately grasp the language and have no problem, and that wasn't the case."[9]

## High School Swagger

Eventually, though, Sergey Brin's proficiency in English improved. He lost his shyness and found himself thriving in the Montessori method. His favorite topics at Paint Branch were puzzles, maps, and math games that taught multiplication. "I really enjoyed the Montessori method," says Brin. "I could grow at my own pace."[10]

From Paint Branch, Brin moved on to Eleanor Roosevelt High School in Baltimore—the type of school where the jocks ruled the campus. (Among the school's graduates are Derrick Williams, a wide receiver for the Detroit Lions, and former National Basketball Association star DeLonte West.) By now, though, Brin was brimming with swagger and self-confidence and was soon recognized as one of the brightest students at school. His academic roster was dominated with college-level classes, enabling him to graduate in 1990 after just three years at Eleanor Roosevelt.

He enrolled at the University of Maryland, where he also graduated after three years. Because of his early graduations from high school and college, he accepted his diploma in 1993 at the age of nineteen—an age when most college students enter their second year of studies. As he prepared to leave the University of Maryland, Brin won a scholarship to study computer science in the graduate school at Stanford University.

## Page: Computers Before Food

While Brin's parents struggled to eke out a living in the repressive Soviet Union, Larry Page enjoyed a much more privileged childhood. Page grew up in a comfortable middle-class neighborhood in Lansing, Michigan. His father, Carl, was a computer science professor at Michigan State University; his mother, Gloria, held a graduate degree in computer science and taught computer programming at Michigan State. Education was always emphasized in the Page home: Page recalls that whenever the family took vacations, they brought an extra suitcase specifically to fill with books they discovered in their travels.

When Larry was eight years old his parents divorced, but Carl and Gloria remained committed to raising Larry and his older brother, Carl Jr., in a healthy environment. When Carl remarried, Larry's stepmother, Joyce Wildenthal, a Michigan State professor, treated the boys as though they were her own children.

From an early age, Larry was exposed to computers. "I was really lucky that my father was a computer science professor, which is unusual for someone my age," he recalls. "We were lucky enough to get our first computer in 1978. It was huge, and it cost a lot of money and we couldn't afford to eat well after that. I always liked computers because I thought you could do a lot with them."[11]

In fact, Page even completed his elementary school homework on the family's home computer, turning in his assignments printed with an old-style dot matrix printer. (A dot matrix printer formed numerical char-

> "We were lucky enough to get our first computer in 1978. It was huge, and it cost a lot of money and we couldn't afford to eat well after that."[11]
>
> —Google cocreator Larry Page.

acters or letters of the alphabet by imprinting the page with tiny dots.) At the time, many of his teachers had never even seen a computer printout.

Page's interest in technology was not limited to computers. He was constantly tinkering with the appliances in his home, taking them apart and putting them back together just to see how they worked. Later, as a student at East Lansing High School, Page built a working inkjet printer—out of Lego blocks.

## Influenced by Tesla

When he was twelve years old, Page discovered a biography of Nikola Tesla, the nineteenth-century Serbian-born American inventor who developed much of the science that is employed in modern electric motors. Tesla also pioneered ways to use electricity as an energy source. However, Tesla never profited from his inventions—his investors shortchanged him, and he was occasionally forced to take jobs as a manual laborer to pay his bills. Page read the book *Prodigal Genius: The Life of Nikola Tesla* by John Joseph O'Neill cover to cover. "I found it very sad," Page recalls. "You can imagine if he were slightly more skilled in business, or with people, he'd have gotten a lot more done."[12]

By now Page had decided on his own life's course: He would be an inventor. But the Tesla biography had made a big impression on him—he knew he would have to be savvy in business as well. "I realized I wanted to invent things," Page says, "but I also wanted to change the world. . . . [Inventing things] wasn't any

*At age twelve, Larry Page discovered a biography of Nikola Tesla (pictured), the nineteenth-century inventor who developed much of the science that is used in modern electric motors. Tesla's life story and achievements impressed Page, who decided he also wanted to be an inventor.*

good; you really had to get them into the world and have people use them to have any effect. So probably when I was 12, I knew I was going to start a company eventually."[13]

## Stellar Career at Michigan

As did Brin, Page also attended a Montessori school. He then entered East Lansing High School in 1987. If there was one area of interest that rivaled Page's devotion to math and science, it was music. He was a talented saxophone player and, following his freshman year at East Lansing, was chosen to attend a summer music program at the prestigious Interlochen Arts Academy in northern Michigan.

Page graduated from East Lansing in 1991 and entered the University of Michigan that fall. His father, a graduate of the University of Michigan, insisted that his younger son enroll in the school. Says Page, "My dad actually said to me when I was deciding what school to go to, 'We'll pay for any school you want to go to—as long as it's Michigan.'"[14]

"Larry just stood out; he was always ahead. Larry used a handheld computer for his project in my course, before anyone knew what a handheld computer even was."[16]

—University of Michigan engineering professor Elliot Soloway.

Page majored in engineering and excelled in his classes: He was elected president of the university's chapter of Eta Kappa Nu, the national honor society for engineering and computer science students. But mindful of what he had read about Tesla, he also took many courses in business. While at the university, Page enrolled in a leadership training course with a thought-provoking motto: "Have a healthy disregard for the impossible."[15] Elliot Soloway, an electrical engineering professor who taught Page at the university, recalls that Page came to his class equipped with an early version of a tablet computer. "Larry just stood out; he was always ahead," says Soloway. "Larry used a handheld computer for his project in my course, before anyone knew what a handheld computer even was."[16] When not taking classes or participating in leadership training seminars, Page worked in a campus doughnut shop.

In his final year at the University of Michigan, Page traveled to Stanford University for a tour with an eye toward enrolling in the graduate

## How Music Influenced Larry Page and Google

When Larry Page and Sergey Brin developed the Google search engine, they wanted to ensure users would receive results almost instantaneously. Speed and timing were emphasized in the development of Google, largely because Page realized the importance of timing when he learned to play the saxophone as a child. "In some sense I feel like music training led to the high-speed legacy of Google for me," Page says. "In music you're very cognizant of time. Time is like the primary thing. . . . If you think about it from a music point of view, if you're a percussionist, you hit something, it's got to happen in milliseconds, fractions of a second."

During the development of Google, Page constantly pushed the engineers to make it work faster—to return results to the users within seconds, if not milliseconds, of their requests. In fact, the reason the Google home page features little more than the word *Google* can be attributed to Page's obsession with time—he found that if the home page was required to load extensive graphics and illustrations, it would slow down the speed of the searches.

Years after leaving high school, Page continues to maintain an interest in music. In 2012 he took up the drums. "The last couple of years I've been trying to learn percussion a bit, which has been challenging," he said in 2014.

Quoted in Michael Helft, "How Music Education Influenced Larry Page," *Fortune*, November 18, 2014. http://fortune.com.

computer science program. That is where he met Brin, who, although the same age, was already enrolled in the graduate computer science school and served as Page's tour guide. During the tour, Page made conversation with Brin and found himself harboring an immediate dislike for his guide. "Sergey is pretty social; he likes meeting people," says Page. "I thought he was pretty obnoxious. He really had strong opinions about things, and I guess I did, too."[17] For his part, Brin shared that opinion of Page: "We both found each other obnoxious. But we say it a little jokingly. Obviously, we spent a lot of time talking to each other, so there was something there. We had kind of a bantering thing going."[18]

## A Shared Interest

Page ultimately elected to enroll in Stanford, beginning classes in the fall of 1995. As he searched for a topic for his doctoral project, Page was drawn to the still very young World Wide Web and wondered whether the search engines of the era could be improved.

By now Brin was in his third year at Stanford. He intended to earn a PhD but had not yet settled on a topic of study. Instead, Brin decided to enjoy all that Northern California had to offer, devoting himself largely to leisure-time activities. He learned to sail and took up gymnastics—even taking lessons on the trapeze. As for a topic of study, he was in no rush. By now he had been mulling over the idea of making personal movie reviews available on the Internet. Under Brin's plan, people who wrote similar reviews would be drawn to each other's critiques and receive recommendations from one another on other films they may enjoy. (Although Brin ultimately did not pursue the project, other computer science engineers took up the issue, and eventually such a system became available for movies, as well as books, through the online retailer Amazon.)

Instead, Brin developed an interest in mining data from the web—a subject similar to Page's topic. By now the two students had put their original animosity aside and, finding themselves with a common interest, agreed to work together on a project that would revolutionize the task of organizing the enormous amount of information available to billions of people on the Internet.

# Chapter 2

# How Brin and Page Revolutionized Internet Searching

**S**ergey Brin and Larry Page did not invent the Internet search engine. Years before Google went live, users had tools available to help them dig through the growing mountains of data that were accumulating in cyberspace. By using the early search engines, users were able to find information relating to their queries, but the data could be overwhelming. Picking through the volumes of information turned up by the early search engines for specific facts could be time-consuming, cumbersome, and often futile.

It took more than twenty years for the first search engine to become available to users after the Internet went live in 1969. Today it is hard to imagine that the Internet of the twenty-first century—a huge resource of information that provides mountains of text as well as images, video, and audio resources—began life as a very modest project. In 1969 the Advanced Research Projects Agency Network (ARPANET) was created by the US Department of Defense as a system for military computers to share information. Until that time, it was cumbersome to transfer information from computer to computer. Prior to the birth of ARPANET, the most common form of data transfer involved copying information from a computer's hard drive onto a floppy disk, which could then be inserted into another computer. To transfer data from a computer in one city to a computer in another city, the floppy disk had to be mailed—a process that could take several days.

ARPANET was formed to find a way to transfer data instantaneously and without the need to swap floppy disks. The agency enlisted the Computer Science Department at Stanford University to find the answer. Engineers at Stanford resolved to connect computers by telephone lines and transfer information the same way voices are carried from phone to phone (at least, the way voices were transmitted in the pre–cell phone era.) At 10:30 p.m. on October 29, 1969, a computer at the University of California, Los Angeles (UCLA) employed telephone lines to communicate with a computer at Stanford, approximately 370 miles (595 km) away. The first message transmitted by the UCLA computer was composed by engineering professor Leonard Kleinrock, assisted by student Charley Kline. The message was supposed to be the word *login*, but the computer crashed before the full word was typed. Therefore, the first piece of information to appear in cyberspace was the word *lo*. (After the crash, the UCLA computer was rebooted, and the word *login* was re-sent—this time successfully.) Nevertheless, despite that early stumble the Internet had been born.

## Archie Searches the Internet

ARPANET grew slowly. By 1977 there were 111 computers connected on ARPANET, sharing information without the need to swap floppy disks. By 1984 the number had grown to 1,000. By then the government had opened ARPANET to nonmilitary purposes, and many universities and large corporations made use of the resource. In 1990 ARPANET was officially dissolved as the Internet started taking on the characteristics familiar to today's users.

In fact, by 1990 the question of how to find information on the Internet was gaining interest among computer engineers as well as engineering students. That year, Alan Emtage, a student at McGill University in Montreal, Canada, developed what is regarded as the first Internet search engine. He gave it the highly appropriate name Archives, but early Internet users soon dropped the *v* and *s* from the word and nicknamed the search engine Archie—a tribute to the girl-crazy teenager familiar to millions of comic book and newspaper comic strip readers.

To conduct a search through Archie, users entered keywords into a search bar—much as they do today. Archie responded by creating a directory of

> "[Archie] represented a first effort to [rein] in a quickly growing, chaotic, information resource, not by imposing order on it from above, but by mapping and indexing the disorder to make it more usable."[19]
>
> —Alexander Halavais, an Arizona State University professor and former president of the Association of Internet Researchers.

## Growth of the ARPANET

UWASH · AMES16 · USGS3 · BERK · SILAB · LBL · LLL · UTAH · SAC · ANL · PURDUE · UWISC · RADC · LINCOLN · MIT77 · MIT44 · MIT6 · CCA · AFGL · RCC 5 · RCC 49 · BBN40 · BBN63 · BBN72 · HARVARD · UROCH · NYU · DEC · WPAFD · JOHNS · CORADCOM · ARADCOM · NSWC · CMU · NRL · USGS1 · DARCOM · ABERDEEN · NBS · NSA · DCEC · SDAC · MITRE · CSS · ARPA · NRL · LONDON · PENTAGON · BRAGG · ROBINS · EGLIN · GUNTER · BROOKS · WSMR · AFWL · SANDIA · COLLINS · REDSTONE · SCOTT · OTI · STLA · LOS ALAMOS · USGS2 · TEXAS · YUMA · UCLA · NOSC · ACCAT · CHINA · CT · RAND · USC · ISI27 · AFSD · ISI22 · ISI103 · ISI52 · HICKAM · KOREA · HAWAII · SRI151 · SRI173 · XEROX · TYMS · NPS · SUMEX · STANFORD · DAVID · NIH · UDEL · ANDREW

**1983**

*Although modest by today's standards, the ARPANET represented a huge accomplishment in computer connectivity. By 1983 hundreds of computer users across the United States could share information without having to swap floppy disks.*

sites that included those keywords. The search could be cumbersome—to access a site uncovered by Archie, users had to retype the Internet address produced by the search. And if the information the user sought was not available at the site, the user had to go back to the original Archie results page and type in the next address. This process was repeated until the user unearthed the information he or she needed—if, in fact, that information was found at all. Alexander Halavais, an Arizona State University professor and former president of the Association of Internet Researchers, says:

> It is probably a stretch to say that [Archie] "crawled" these sites, since unlike today's web crawlers it did not . . . examine the full content of each of these pages, but limited itself to the titles of the files. Nevertheless, it represented a first effort to [rein] in a quickly growing, chaotic, information resource, not by imposing order on it from above, but by mapping and indexing the disorder to make it more usable.[19]

# The Information Superhighway

A year after Archie debuted, software engineers produced two improved versions—one known as Veronica (named for Archie's girlfriend), the other Jughead (named for Archie's lazy buddy.) Veronica made more of the Internet accessible to search, while Jughead created links to the search sites, which saved users the chore of retyping the Internet addresses. But there was still a major drawback: Archie, Veronica, and Jughead were still simply searching for keywords without distinguishing whether the information unearthed by the search could truly be helpful to the user.

Meanwhile, the Internet was growing. In the early years of the Internet, it was certainly true that Archie, Veronica, and Jughead had their limitations—but on the other hand, there was relatively little information to comb through. Most of the information contained on the Internet was of a technical nature, drawing interest largely from the engineering and scientific communities. By 1993 there were just 130 nontechnical Internet sites in existence.

But as retailers and other businesses, organizations, governments, schools, and even individuals realized the potential of the Internet, cyberspace exploded with information. In 1994 Congress passed legislation originally written by Senator Al Gore of Tennessee—who was by then the US vice president—requiring competing telecommunications companies to make their telephone lines and microwave signals universally available to the Internet. The legislation recognized the Internet as a public resource that should not be blocked for business purposes. In a 1994 speech, Gore was the first to label the Internet the "information superhighway," saying, "We will create an affirmative obligation to interconnect and to afford nondiscriminatory access to network facilities, services, functions and information. . . . There must be public access to the information superhighway."[20] As Gore had predicted, the Internet saw enormous growth, and when it did it became obvious to Internet users that a better way had to be found to search the Internet than what Archie, Veronica, and Jughead were capable of providing.

> "There must be public access to the information superhighway."[20]
>
> —Former US vice president Al Gore.

In a 1994 speech, US vice president Al Gore (pictured) described the Internet as an "information superhighway"—a phrase that stuck. As Gore predicted, the Internet experienced rapid growth.

## Flaws in the System

By 1996 some six hundred thousand websites had been created. As the Internet grew in size, software engineers developed alternatives to Archie, Veronica, and Jughead. Search engines with names such as InfoSeek, AltaVista, Galaxy, Lycos, WebCrawler, and LookSmart were developed.

All of these search engines improved on Archie and the others in that they ranked websites according to how relevant they were to people who explored the Internet. In other words, if a lot of users were accessing the sites, then InfoSeek, AltaVista, and other search engines presumed their information was of much more value and awarded those sites higher rankings in the search results.

Brin and Page saw the deficiencies in the system: Just because a lot of people were using the same search words and were being led to the same websites did not mean the information was valuable for their individual needs. Moreover, even at this early stage in the life of the Internet, clever entrepreneurs found ways to exploit Internet searching to their advantage. By repeating the same searches hundreds of times, using the same keywords and then clicking on the same pages, these entrepreneurs could create the false impression that these pages were popular and valuable sources of information. But in reality all they were really doing was fooling the existing search engines into believing these sites received a lot of traffic. Says Page, "[Existing search engines] were looking only at text and not considering [other factors]."[21]

## Making the Internet User-Friendly

At Stanford, Brin and Page discovered the book *The Design of Everyday Things* by Donald A. Norman. It was Norman's contention that manufacturers rarely designed their products with the consumer in mind. Instead, products were designed so the company could make them as cheaply as possible, thereby realizing the largest profit possible. That is why consumer products—from cameras to phones to kitchen appliances—often take a frustratingly long time for consumers to figure out how to use. (The term *user-friendly* is believed to have originated in the early 1980s, but by the 1990s the concept had still not found traction among a large number of manufacturers serving consumers.) Page found himself particularly intrigued by the concept—he recalled staying in a hotel room and spending several minutes trying to figure out how to turn on the lights in his room.

Page and Brin believed the concept of *user-friendly* should apply to Internet searching. In 1996 they began work on an algorithm—a mathematical formula that drives software—that assessed the number of links other websites maintained to particular sites. This suggested to Page and Brin that the administrators of those sites believed the links led their users to valuable information. Therefore, instead of relying simply on keywords and volume of user traffic to lead users to the information they seek, the system developed by Page and Brin also relied on how many times the websites were linked to other websites.

This was a major breakthrough because all websites contain information—but search engines could not tell users how good that information might be. Brin and Page figured out that the site administrators who were linking their pages to other sites were acting as judges, essentially telling people where to find good information. In other words, the same keywords could conceivably be found on pages created by tech giants such as Apple or Microsoft as well as on pages created by teenage programmers testing their skills by creating live pages on the web. However, when site administrators created links on their pages to other sites they regarded as valuable resources, chances are they referred their visitors to sites maintained by the likes of Apple and Microsoft—and not by teenagers sharpening their website-building skills. These were the links Brin and Page were anxious to identify and reward by ranking them high in their search engine page results. Says Page, "We realized that we had a querying tool. It gave you a good overall ranking of pages and ordering of follow-up pages."[22]

## Wisdom of Crowds

This was, in reality, not a new concept. Essentially, Page and Brin were relying on the "wisdom of crowds," a well-grounded belief that the collective opinion of a large group of people is wiser than an idea put forth by a single individual.

Brin and Page called their system PageRank—something of a tongue-in-cheek title, given the name of one of the developers of the algorithm. Still, that is what the program accomplished—it ranked web pages according to how many times they were linked to other pages.

PageRank was developed between 1996 and 1998, when its details were finally written down in a paper by Brin and Page. When that paper was released, PageRank reflected tremendous foresight by the two Stanford students about where they thought the Internet was heading. Again, in 1996 there were still relatively few websites—no more than six hundred thousand. But Page and Brin knew the Internet was on the

## How to Use PageRank

Two decades after Larry Page and Sergey Brin wrote the algorithm PageRank, the mathematical formula continues to drive the Google software. Moreover, Google has established tools for users to see how PageRank works. When a user wishes to discover the links connected to a specific website, the user must first install the Google toolbar (available at www.google.com/toolbar) on a web browser. Once the toolbar is installed, the user clicks on the wrench icon at the top right corner of the page.

That action opens a box. The user then clicks on the Privacy tab and finds the box for Enhanced features. To turn on PageRank, the user checks the box for PageRank. That creates a small green box in the Google toolbar. To find the links connected to the page, the user clicks on the green box and then the link for Backward Pages.

A 2015 PageRank search for the links connected to the website Coolmath .com uncovered more than three hundred links. The page was established to help young people study mathematics. Many of the pages linked to Coolmath .com were established by the administrators of websites for American schools, indicating that many math teachers found Coolmath.com a valuable resource for their students and linked their school pages to the site.

verge of a huge expansion of information, and they knew there had to be a better way to organize that information for users than simply relying on keywords and traffic. "They understood one big thing," says technology journalist Ken Auletta. "They were establishing a formula that would harness the growth of their search engine to the growth of the Web."[23]

## Debut of BackRub

At the time Brin and Page were developing PageRank, their initial idea was to employ it as the driving component behind a search engine known as BackRub. The name was a reference to the purpose of the search engine:

to follow the links *back* to the original source, thus ranking the source according to the number of links generated by the source's administrator. BackRub made its debut in March 1996. The logo for BackRub, a handprint, was conceived by Page. In fact, it was Page's handprint. To compose the logo, he placed his hand on the glass table of a digital scanner and scanned an image of his hand. To compose the logo, he converted the image into a negative rendering. The entire process took a few seconds.

The first search conducted on BackRub was performed by Page, and he entered keywords searching for his personal website. All Stanford computer engineering students were required to compose their own websites—essentially providing biographical information, favorite books, their areas of study at Stanford, and similar details about their lives.

By 1997 BackRub was in wide use among Stanford students. By now, though, Page and Brin had changed their minds about the name of their search engine. They simply did not think BackRub was a catchy name.

> "[Brin and Page] understood one big thing. They were establishing a formula that would harness the growth of their search engine to the growth of the Web."[23]
>
> —Technology journalist Ken Auletta.

## Name Conceived in Error

They would, of course, rename their search engine Google, but the name was actually conceived in error. Moreover, it was another Stanford graduate student, Sean Anderson, and not Page or Brin who thought up the name.

Anderson recalls that Brin and Page had been kicking around several candidates for the name and were not satisfied with any of their ideas. On September 15, 1997, Anderson, who shared an office with Page, started tossing in his own ideas. Recalls Anderson:

> I would go to the whiteboard and start brainstorming and [Page] would say, "No, no, no." . . . He started getting desperate, and we had another brainstorming session. I was sitting at the whiteboard and one of the last things I came up with was, "How about Googleplex?" I said, "You are trying to come up with a [search engine] that searches and indexes and allows people to organize vast amounts of data. Googleplex is a huge number." He liked that.[24]

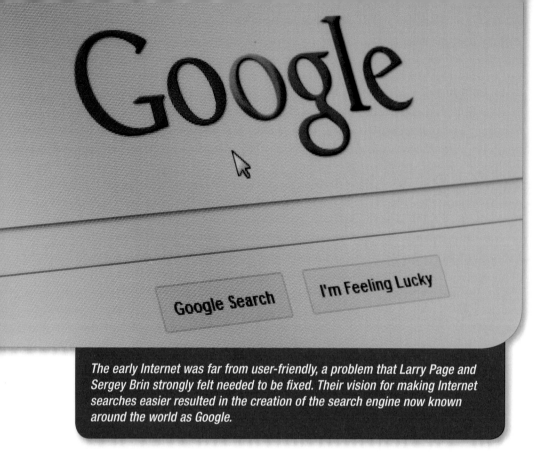

The early Internet was far from user-friendly, a problem that Larry Page and Sergey Brin strongly felt needed to be fixed. Their vision for making Internet searches easier resulted in the creation of the search engine now known around the world as Google.

In fact, though, Anderson was wrong. The correct word and spelling for the term Anderson thought he had suggested is *googol*. A googol is a numeral written as a 1 followed by 100 zeroes.

Page, who did not realize Anderson was in error, was nevertheless intrigued. Anderson recalls, "He said, 'How about we try Google?' He liked it shorter." Anderson then entered the URL *www.Google.com* into his Internet browser and discovered it was available as a domain address. Says Anderson, "Larry found that acceptable, and he registered it later that evening and wrote it on the whiteboard: Google.com. It had a wild Internet ring to it, like Yahoo or Amazon."[25]

The next day, Anderson found a note left on his desk by another Stanford graduate student, Tamara Munzner, advising Anderson that in concocting the new name for BackRub, he and Page had misspelled googol. Anderson performed a quick Internet search for the URL *www.Googol .com* and learned it was already in existence, meaning it was unavailable for Brin and Page. (Today www.Googol.com is no longer in existence—

visitors who type in the URL are redirected to a page sponsored by a mathematics tutoring organization.)

## Billions of Links

Despite the misspelling, to Page and Brin the new name was appropriate. In the fall of 1997, when BackRub became Google, the amount of information available on the Internet was still relatively small, but Brin

## BackRub and Its "Borrowed" Equipment

The first headquarters for the BackRub search engine was Larry Page's dorm room at Stanford University. The tiny room was crammed with computer equipment—most of it borrowed. In fact, as they developed BackRub, Page and Sergey Brin snuck onto a loading dock at Stanford where new computers had just been delivered. They helped themselves to what they needed, even bringing their own cart to transport the hardware back to Page's room. And when Page could not fit any more equipment in his room, they started outfitting Brin's room with hardware.

In 1996 and 1997, as BackRub went into development, it was no secret around the Stanford campus what was going on in the dorm rooms of Page and Brin. But Stanford professors and administrators permitted the students to use whatever resources they required, knowing Brin and Page were working on a project that could revolutionize Internet search. "We're lucky there were a lot of forward-looking people at Stanford," Page says. "They didn't hassle us too much about the resources we were using."

Brin and Page were using not only Stanford's hardware but also the storage space in the university's mainframe—the central database of all information stored in the university's computers. BackRub, which was searching the entire Internet for links that connected websites to websites, occasionally caused problems with the Stanford computer network. "We caused the whole Stanford network to go down," says Page.

Quoted in John Battelle, "The Birth of Google," *Wired*, August 2005. http://archive.wired.com.

Quoted in Ken Auletta, *Googled: The End of the World as We Know It*. New York: Penguin, 2009, p. 39.

and Page knew it would continue to grow. And as each new website was added to the Internet, more links would be created. Eventually, they believed, the number of links their search engine would be asked to rank would total in the billions—a number that would not approach the size of a googol, certainly, but still representing an unfathomable amount of information that Brin and Page were certain their search engine could track, organize, and make available to users.

# Chapter 3

# Turning Google into Big Business

Stanford University is located near the city of Palo Alto in the heart of California's so-called Silicon Valley where, since the 1970s, many of the top high-tech companies in the nation have established their headquarters. Located just south of San Francisco, Silicon Valley is home to the computer makers Apple and Hewlett-Packard. Other companies headquartered in Silicon Valley are Cisco Systems, which among its many enterprises develops hardware and software that enable computers to connect on the Internet, and Oracle, which provides hardware and software that help corporate clients manage the information stored in their databases.

Many of the engineers and executives who work in Silicon Valley have been recruited from Stanford's computer science school and maintain close ties to the institution. As Page and Brin were developing PageRank and Google, word spread quickly through Silicon Valley that the two Stanford students were onto something big.

The first former Stanford graduate to recognize the potential of Google was Andy Bechtolsheim, founder of a company known then as Sun Microsystems, which developed hardware and software for a number of computer applications. (Oracle acquired Sun Microsystems in 2010.) In 1998 a Stanford professor, David Cheriton, suggested to Brin and Page that they contact Bechtolsheim and ask for financial backing for Google. That night Brin sent Bechtolsheim an e-mail requesting a meeting. Bechtolsheim replied immediately, suggesting they meet at eight o'clock the next morning.

*Andy Bechtolsheim, founder of the hardware and software development company Sun Microsystems, was an early and important supporter of Google. After a brief demonstration of Page and Brin's search engine, Bechtolsheim handed them a $100,000 check.*

The meeting occurred on the porch of Cheriton's Palo Alto home. Using Cheriton's laptop, Brin and Page demonstrated the capabilities of Google. After watching the brief demonstration, Bechtolsheim said, "Well, I don't want to waste time. I'm sure it will help you guys if I just write a check."[26] And then Bechtolsheim took out his checkbook and wrote a check to Brin and Page for $100,000.

## Profiting from Their Research

In the fall of 1997, when Brin and Page changed the name of their search engine from BackRub to Google, they had decided to take their project to the next step—to establish it as a business. Initially, Brin and Page had no intentions of making BackRub—or its eventual successor—into a private company. Their intention was to develop PageRank and BackRub as a project to obtain their doctoral degrees in computer science at Stanford.

But Page recalled the lessons he had learned in reading the biography of Nikola Tesla and realized that if their research did revolutionize Internet search, they had to ensure they would profit from the venture. In 1997, as BackRub was under development, Jon Kleinberg, a noted computer engineer for tech giant IBM, visited the Stanford campus and was shown BackRub by Page.

In his conversation with Page, Kleinberg says, the student made it very clear he feared he would suffer a similar fate as Tesla—that he would spearhead an important scientific breakthrough but realize no financial gain. "He was concerned that someone might steal his ideas,"[27] says Kleinberg.

## Dropping Out of Stanford

Bechtolsheim's investment enabled Brin and Page to incorporate Google as a private company. In September 1998 they moved out of their Stanford dorm rooms and set up their own company—and in doing so, both students dropped out of school. Brin and Page had enrolled at Stanford to pursue doctoral degrees in computer science, but neither would be awarded degrees. By devoting all their energies toward the development and growth of Google, neither founder had the time to complete the work required to obtain his degree.

Google's first headquarters was the Menlo Park, California, garage of Susan Wojcicki, an engineer at computer-chip maker Intel and the former college roommate of Brin's ex-girlfriend. (Later, Wojcicki joined the Google staff and eventually rose to the presidency of YouTube, which Google acquired in 2006.) Working in these modest circumstances, Page and Brin continued to modify Google, sharpening the PageRank algorithm so that it could do a better job of identifying links and ranking pages under the "wisdom of crowds" concept.

It was a job Brin and Page could not do alone. Within a few weeks of moving into Wojcicki's garage, Brin and Page started hiring employees—mostly graduates of Stanford's computer science school. By late 1998

Google employed seven engineers—all working in Wojcicki's garage as well as two spare rooms in her basement. "They were there at all times of the day and night,"[28] she says. The Google staff members were, however, very considerate tenants. When one of their employees' cars was in need of a muffler replacement, Brin, Page, and the other staff members pushed the car to the end of the street before the owner started the ignition—in consideration of Wojcicki and her neighbors, who would have objected to the car's noisy engine.

Making use of Bechtolsheim's investment, Brin and Page paid Wojcicki rent of $1,700 a month. For a company that would eventually be worth billions of dollars, the early days of Google were quite modest. Brin, Page, and their employees worked at folding tables or even on plywood sheets laid across wooden sawhorses. They kept the garage door open to provide ventilation. On the outside of the garage door they posted a sign that read: "Google World Headquarters."[29]

> "The site has an uncanny knack for returning extremely relevant results. There's much more to come at Google, but even in its prototype form it's a great search engine."[30]
>
> — 1998 review in *PC Magazine*.

## The Buzz on Google

At this point, Google was still a little-known resource on the web. In 1998 the Internet marketing company comScore reported that four search engines were among the top twenty most popular websites: these search engines were Excite, Lycos, InfoSeek, and AltaVista. Nevertheless, although Google was still a little-used resource for conducting Internet searches, technology insiders saw value in Google's concept and the potential for Google to dominate Internet search. In 1998 *PC Magazine* had this to say about Google: "The site has an uncanny knack for returning extremely relevant results. There's much more to come at Google, but even in its prototype form it's a great search engine."[30]

Indeed, the buzz surrounding Google was circulating among the top investors in Silicon Valley. By June 1999 Brin and Page had raised more than $25 million in funds known as venture capital—investments by forward-thinking entrepreneurs who are more prone to investing in ideas than in proven products or services. This infusion of cash enabled Page

## The Google Logo

Thanks to Google's enormous popularity as a search engine, the company's logo is one of the most familiar corporate symbols in the world. The very simple logo, featuring the word *Google* in red, blue, green, and yellow characters, was originally designed in 1998 by Sergey Brin using a free graphic arts program named GIMP. Brin's design included an exclamation point at the end of the word.

In 1999, thanks to the infusion of cash by investors, Brin and Larry Page had the resources to have the logo professionally redesigned. Brin and Page hired Ruth Kedar, a graduate of Stanford University's graphic design school, to redesign the logo. By then Brin and Page had decided to drop the exclamation point. However, they insisted that Brin's original concept be maintained because the two founders liked its simplicity and wanted the Google home page to remain uncluttered by graphic elements. According to Kedar, the most challenging part of the job was finding the right typeface. She says:

> The chosen typeface is a based on Catull, an old style . . . typeface. Catull borrows elements from traditional writing instruments such as the quill and the chisel with a modern twist. Search, by nature, is an activity that requires we look into the past. Therefore Catull's historical ties seemed appropriate, as did the bridging between the old analog world and the new emerging digital era.

Quoted in Philipp Lenssen, "Ruth Kedar on Designing the Google Logo," *Google Blogoscoped*, January 14, 2008. http://blogoscoped.com.

and Brin to move out of Wojcicki's garage and into a second-floor office on University Avenue in Palo Alto, about 1 mile (1.6 km) from the Stanford campus. It was the first of many moves for Google before Brin and Page established the company's permanent headquarters in 2004 in the nearby town of Mountain View.

At this point, Brin and Page had developed a groundbreaking method for searching the Internet. They had attracted investors, hired employees, and leased office space. But they had no idea how they were going to make Google profitable. As far as Page was concerned, once Google became the dominant search engine on the Internet, somebody at the company would figure out a way to earn a profit. "We started this company because we were unhappy with current search technology," Page insisted. "If we are successful, [profitability] will be just a great side effect."[31]

At first, Page's attitude found some traction in Silicon Valley, where many of the other early high-tech companies had been started by entrepreneurs like Brin and Page—engineers who discovered dynamic new ways to exploit the Internet without worrying about how they were going to make money. One of the earliest investors in Google was Jeff Bezos, the founder of Amazon, who met Page and Brin in November 1998 and, like Bechtolsheim, wrote them a check after seeing them demonstrate Google. "I just fell in love with Larry and Sergey,"[32] he says. In fact, when Bezos asked Brin and Page if they had written a business plan—a road map for how they intended to turn Google into a profitable venture—the two founders admitted there was none. Bezos wrote a check anyway. "There was no business plan," he says. "They had a vision. It was a customer-focused point of view."[33]

> "I just fell in love with Larry and Sergey."[32]
>
> —Jeff Bezos, founder of Amazon.

Eventually, though, Brin and Page decided that to make a profit, Google had to become a vehicle for advertising. They came to this conclusion reluctantly, because the notion of running ads on Google was a concept they had originally resisted.

## Banner Ads

Long before the debut of Google, advertisers promoted their products on the Internet. Typically, retailers and others who bought advertising space on a website purchased space as though they were buying advertising space in print newspapers or magazines. These so-called banner ads appeared across the top, bottom, or sides of the screen and provided

Jeff Bezos, the founder of Amazon, was an early investor in Google. He was impressed with Page and Brin's overall vision and with their focus on the user experience.

whatever information the advertiser desired: an image of the product for sale, a description, the price, a website to visit to see more about the product, or a toll-free number to call to order the product. As Internet speeds increased, some advertisers included videos—essentially, TV commercials—in their web-based ads.

But Brin and Page did not immediately agree that advertising had a place on Google. They believed people searching the Internet were entitled to commercial-free experiences and that merchandisers should not be given access to the nature of information people were seeking. In their 1998 Stanford paper providing the technical details for Page-Rank, they asserted, "Currently, the predominant business model for

## Acquiring YouTube

Jawed Karim, Chad Hurley, and Steve Chen were friends and coworkers at PayPal, the online billing service, when they developed YouTube. In 2005 the three men attended a party together and wanted to share video they shot at the gathering, but they discovered there was no easy way to share video files over the Internet. On September 23, 2005, they unveiled YouTube, featuring an eighteen-second video of Karim visiting the San Diego Zoo.

Since then YouTube has become one of the most popular sites on the Internet as millions of amateur and professional videographers have posted their work online. According to 2014 statistics released by YouTube, more than 1 billion unique users visit the site each month, watching more than 6 billion hours of video. Moreover, more than 100 hours of video are uploaded onto YouTube each minute. Given such statistics, YouTube's value as a vehicle for advertising has long been recognized.

In 2006, just a year after YouTube's debut, Sergey Brin and Larry Page announced Google's acquisition of the website from Karim, Hurley, and Chen for $1.65 billion. In announcing the sale, Brin said he saw YouTube as the future of entertainment on the Internet—just as he had envisioned Google as the future of Internet search nearly a decade earlier. He said, "It's hard to imagine a better fit with another company. This really reminds me of Google just a few short years ago."

Quoted in NBC News, "Google Buys YouTube for $1.65 Billion," October 10, 2006. www.nbcnews.com.

commercial search engines is advertising. The goals of the advertising business model do not always correspond to providing quality search to users."[34]

In their paper, they discussed a particular search that could be conducted focusing on the dangers of talking on cell phones while driving. They suggested that during such a search, it would be entirely possible that advertisements for cell phones would stream across the results page as users searched for information on the dangers of using them while driving. "For this type of reason . . . we expect that advertising funded search engines will be inherently biased towards the advertisers and away from the needs of the consumers,"[35] they asserted.

## Pay-per-Click

In addition, Brin and Page liked the simplicity of the Google results page—nothing more than lists of links and brief text highlighting the keywords entered by the users. They found Internet-style banner ads ugly, distracting, and as they pointed out in their 1998 paper, biased toward the advertisers. Says writer Ken Auletta, "Brin and Page resisted ads because they shared an allergy then common among Webheads . . . that advertising was like a rude stranger interrupting a conversation to sell you something you neither wanted nor needed."[36]

On the other hand, by 1999 the venture capitalists financing Google wanted to start seeing profits. Moreover, by now Brin and Page were heading a company employing fifty people. The investors started sending signals to Brin and Page that unless they found a way to start turning a profit, the money tap would be turned off, meaning the Google employees would lose their jobs. "We really couldn't figure out the business model," says Michael Moritz, a Google investor. "There was a period when things were looking pretty bleak."[37]

Reluctantly, Brin and Page accepted the notion that they would have to open Google to advertising. But they set strict limits on what they would accept and how the advertisements would appear. For example, there would be no advertisements for liquor or firearms. And Google would make a special effort to reach out to small businesses. "We don't try to put our sense of ethics into the search results, but we do when it comes to advertising,"[38] says Brin.

Mostly, though, Brin and Page did not want to see banner-style ads popping up on Google search pages. Instead, they elected to adopt a model known as pay-per-click. In designing Google's advertising program, they borrowed heavily from another website, GoTo.com, a rival

> "We really couldn't figure out the business model. There was a period when things were looking pretty bleak."[37]
>
> —Google investor Michael Moritz.

search engine that originated the concept of pay-per-click. GoTo.com was vastly different from other search engines because it was entirely driven by advertising. In other words, the only results that appeared on the search pages were those that had been purchased by advertisers. What was key to the GoTo.com advertising model, though, was the advertiser paid a fee to GoTo.com only when a user clicked on the link.

## Ads Linked to Keywords

On June 26, 2000, Google emerged as the top search engine on the Internet when the company announced that it had surpassed Lycos in user preference and was now hosting some 30 million searches per day. That meant advertisers were guaranteed potentially millions of opportunities per day for customers to see their ads on Google. That October Brin and Page unveiled their version of pay-per-click, calling their advertising model AdWords. The ads appeared as small notices amid the results of a Google search. (Originally, the ads were text-only, but in later years Brin and Page permitted advertisers to include small images with their ads.) The ads appear across the top, side, or bottom of the page—depending on the advertiser's preference—with ads across the top costing more, of course. And the advertisements are clearly labeled as ads—Brin and Page did not want users fooled into thinking they were clicking on informational websites, then finding themselves staring at Internet pages created by retailers.

The ads do not just appear on all Google searches, though. Instead, they are linked directly to the keyword searches conducted by the users. The user still receives a menu of relevant websites based on the keywords entered into the search, but chances are that AdWords advertisements will also appear on the screen.

For example, if a user searches for a ski resort in Vermont—entering the keywords "skiing," "resort" and "Vermont"—websites for Vermont ski resorts are listed on the search page. However, if a ski shop in Vermont is participating in the AdWords program, a small text-only advertisement

AdWords, Google's advertising model, guaranteed companies millions of opportunities daily for consumers to see their advertisements. Ads appear across the top, side, or bottom of search pages, promoting products or services related to user searches.

for that ski shop appears on the results page as well. With AdWords, the Vermont ski shop owner is guaranteed that people planning a skiing trip to Vermont would see the ad, which could possibly lead to sales.

Moreover, in adopting the pay-per-click model, Google did not simply charge for ad space on the search page—much as a website or print publication might charge for space for a banner ad. Rather, Google charged by the click—meaning every time a Google user performed a mouse click on the advertisement for the Vermont ski shop, the retailer was assessed a charge.

AdWords proved to be enormously successful. In 2001 the venture capitalists finally saw a return on their investments as Google turned its first profit—$7 million, a paltry sum given the multibillion-dollar values of most Silicon Valley high-tech companies. But that profit jumped to $100 million in 2002 after Google introduced AdWords Select, a unique concept in which advertisers bid on keywords. In other words, Google auctioned off keywords to advertisers, who bought the rights to have their AdWords boxes appear on search pages in which those keywords are used. "It was instant gold,"[39] says technology writer Will Oremus.

## Rewarding Innovation

Google was now on its way to becoming one of the most profitable companies in American history. From that rather modest start in Wojcicki's garage, Google—thanks largely to those tiny ads that appear on the website's search pages—reported a profit of some $13 billion in 2013.

In 2004 Google became a public corporation—meaning that Brin and Page agreed to sell shares of stock on the NASDAQ stock exchange. (The acronym stands for National Association of Securities Dealers Automated Quotations.) It is a stock exchange where shares of high-tech companies are typically bought and sold. In 2004 the opening price offered for a share of Google was eighty-five dollars. Investors eagerly bought up the shares, and in the more than a decade since Google has been a public corporation, the price of its shares has continually risen, indicating that investors feel the company continues to hold great promise. In early 2015 Google's shares were valued at more than $500 each. For Page and Brin, the value that investors have placed in Internet search represents a tremendous achievement for the two founders, whose innovation has certainly been richly rewarded.

# Chapter 4

# Creating a Culture of Creativity

Google has emerged as one of the most unusual companies in the world, largely because Brin and Page have created a culture of creativity in their organization. This culture is evident to any visitor who sets foot on the campus of Google's corporate headquarters, known as the Googleplex.

There are, for example, Google cafés, where employees can eat for free and, more importantly, are encouraged to interact, talk about their projects, and solicit ideas from one another about how to solve problems. Brin and Page have established a company-wide policy known as FixIt, in which a twenty-four-hour period is set aside for all engineers to drop whatever they are doing and focus on solving a specific problem.

Supervisors are constantly evaluated for their performances—not only by their own superiors, but by their employees as well. Top-level management constantly surveys employees to determine whether their supervisors are doing their best to encourage innovation. Laszlo Bock, senior vice president of human resources—known at Google as People Operations—says, "People look for meaning in their work. People want to know what's happening in their environment. People want to have some ability to shape that environment."[40]

Google's dedication to fostering innovation among its employees has paid dividends for the company. Indeed, many of Google's most successful ventures have emerged through unique Google innovation programs. One such program, known as 20 percent time, produced AdSense—an enormously lucrative venture that revolutionized how advertisements appear on websites.

## 20 Percent Time

Unlike AdWords, AdSense advertisements do not appear on the Google search pages but instead on the pages users select from their Google searches. For example, if a user researches a legal issue by using a Google search and is eventually led to a page sponsored by a legal publication, an advertisement for a law firm may pop up on the website.

To make AdSense work, entrepreneurs buy the rights to keywords from Google. Google then serves as a matchmaker, linking AdSense advertisements to the pages where Google searches have led the users. In other words, the person looking for legal advice may have used "medical malpractice" as keywords, prompting the appearance of an advertisement sponsored by a law firm that specializes in medical malpractice cases. That firm's advertisement appeared on the website because the firm bought the rights to the keywords "medical malpractice" from Google.

> "We encourage our employees, in addition to their regular projects, to spend 20 percent of their time working on what they think will most benefit Google. This empowers them to be more creative and innovative."[42]
>
> —Google cocreators Sergey Brin and Larry Page.

As with AdWords, the advertiser pays Google only when the user clicks on the link. According to technology journalist Danny Sullivan, "[AdSense] basically turned the Web into a giant Google billboard. It effectively meant that Google could turn everyone's content into a place for Google ads."[41]

AdSense, which made its debut in 2001, would not have been possible without a decision by Brin and Page to take a step most companies regard as a waste of resources. Soon after founding the company in 1998, Brin and Page established a policy permitting all Google engineers to devote 20 percent of their time—essentially, one day a week—to projects they conceive on their own. Such projects are not assigned by supervisors; instead, employees come up with their own ideas and are given the freedom, and the resources of Google, to pursue them.

Brin and Page saw the program as not only a method to harvest fresh ideas from their engineers but also as a way to attract top talent to Google. They believed that top engineers relish opportunities to work on their own ideas and would flock to Google. In a 2004 letter to their employees, Page and Brin wrote:

We encourage our employees, in addition to their regular projects, to spend 20 percent of their time working on what they think will most benefit Google. This empowers them to be more creative and innovative. Many of our significant advances have happened in this manner. For example, AdSense [was] . . . prototyped in "20 percent time." Most risky projects fizzle, often teaching us something. Others succeed and become attractive businesses.[42]

Employees at Google headquarters in Mountain View, California, work in a relaxed setting. The company's founders are dedicated to fostering employee innovation through a culture of creativity.

## The Birth of Gmail

AdSense was conceived by Google engineer Paul Buchheit. His idea, and the time he was permitted to devote to developing the AdSense model, serves as proof that Brin and Page made a profitable decision in giving their employees tremendous freedom to pursue their own ideas. In 2012 AdSense earned some $13 billion for Google.

In addition to AdSense, another project produced by Buchheit during 20 percent time is Gmail, the e-mail service available to virtually everyone. Gmail made its debut in 2004. People with Gmail accounts are able to organize their e-mail messages differently than people who maintain e-mail accounts through other services. Other e-mail accounts enable people to save their old e-mails in folders; Gmail enables users to label their saved mails. By attaching labels to e-mails, Gmail users can drop the same e-mail message into several folders and also attach personal reminders such as "read later" or "from a friend." These labels help users find old e-mails they may need to reference—perhaps after several years of storage. According to authors David A. Vise and Mark Malseed, "Larry and Sergey wanted to make a big splash with Gmail. There was no reason to provide the service unless it was radically better than email services already offered by Microsoft, Yahoo, AOL, and others. . . . For example, it was difficult, if not impossible, to find and retrieve old emails when users needed them."[43]

Other projects developed by Google staff members during 20 percent time include Google News, which leads users to breaking news stories based on keyword searches; Google Talk, an instant messaging service that provides users access to voice and text communications; and Google Transit, an Internet-based service that enables travelers to plan trips using public transportation.

## The Googleplex

These innovations were spawned at a unique complex of buildings in Mountain View that serves as Google's headquarters. The Googleplex is a 3-million-square-foot (278,709 sq. m) complex located on 68 acres (27.5 ha), providing offices and computer labs for some eight thousand of Google's nineteen thousand employees. The other Googlers, as Google

## The Internship

Filmgoers received a behind-the-scenes look at the Googleplex thanks to the 2013 comedy *The Internship*, starring Vince Vaughn and Owen Wilson. The movie, which was filmed partly on the Google campus, tells the story of a couple of unemployed salesmen, Billy (Vaughn) and Nick (Wilson), who land coveted internships at Google. Billy and Nick know virtually nothing about computers or technology, but they have a lot common sense, which they pass on to the young tech-savvy summer interns with whom they are teamed at Google.

In her review of the film, Associated Press movie critic Jocelyn Noveck praised the performances of Vaughn and Wilson but said the real star of *The Internship* is the Googleplex. "It is never once questioned that this is the ultimate place to work," wrote Noveck. "From the free food to the nap pods to the driverless cars to the adult-sized slides, and the always sunny days, this is the Shangri-La of the corporate world."

Google cofounder Sergey Brin makes two brief appearances in the film. At one point, Brin is filmed riding a bicycle in the background of a scene. The director, Shawn Levy, said he did not even know it was Brin when the camera panned across the Google campus, catching Brin on his bike. Later in the film, Brin plays himself to congratulate Billy and Nick on landing full-time jobs at Google. Cofounder Larry Page declined Levy's invitation to appear on camera.

Jocelyn Noveck, "Review: Vaughn-Wilson's *Internship* Silly but Fun," Associated Press Worldstream, June 5, 2013.

employees are known, work in some seventy other locations in more than fifty countries.

Any visitor entering the Googleplex is soon struck by the realization that the facility is like few other corporate headquarters on the planet. Indeed, there are many oddities found on the Googleplex campus that are not normally found on the grounds of major American corporations.

For example, upon entering the campus, visitors encounter a statue depicting a *Tyrannosaurus rex* skeleton. Brin and Page bought the statue from the property's former owners—a computer graphics company that created the special effects for the 1993 film *Jurassic Park*, which told the story of dinosaurs brought to life. The tyrannosaur, nicknamed Stan, sits on the campus to serve as a not-so-subtle reminder to staffers to maintain their creativity and not permit the company to fall into extinction—like a dinosaur.

Bicycles are seemingly everywhere—that is how Brin and Page encourage their employees to travel from building to building. Those who are not biking are jogging—physical fitness is stressed at the company, and Googlers have free use of an on-site gym and pool. Journalist Lance Ulanoff, who visited the Googleplex, reported, "Touring the campus … I saw everything from a full-sized T-Rex skeleton replica to vegetable gardens to a volleyball court. In each building, Google seems to promote fitness and your overall well-being. There are rock-climbing walls, massage chairs, and helmets for use with any of the dozens of Google bikes scattered around campus."[44]

## TGIF Meetings

There are also many cafeterias on the campus—and all the food is free. Ulanoff says common sense would dictate that giving employees access to free food would encourage obesity, but at the Googleplex, that is not the case. During his tour, Ulanoff noted that most employees seemed to be physically fit. "All the food is free, yet none of the employees I saw were fat or even a little bit overweight," he says. "Perhaps that has something to do with the full-service gym. It has it all, including stationary bikes, climbing machines, and an endless pool, complete with lifeguard."[45]

In fact, Brin and Page have even hired physicians to work at the Googleplex. "We have doctors on site," says Page. "We'd like to do more of that where we really make health care convenient and easy and faster, which I think helps people stay healthy. If your access to health care involves your leaving work and driving somewhere and parking and waiting for a long time, that's not going to promote healthiness."[46]

Most of the buildings on the Googleplex feature floor-to-ceiling windows; the interior walls are painted in bright primary colors. Brin and

Page believe sunlight and bright colors enhance creativity. Once a week Brin and Page make themselves available to any Google employee who chooses to attend TGIF meetings. (*TGIF* is an old expression often uttered by frazzled employees who are glad the workweek has finally come to an end—it means "thank God it's Friday.") Even the newest Google employees, known on the campus as Nooglers, are encouraged to attend and pose questions directly to the company's founders.

The meetings were originally held on Fridays but in 2012 were moved to Thursdays so that Google employees based in Asia could participate via Internet streaming—many Asian cities are in time zones eight hours ahead of the American West Coast. Holding the meetings on Fridays forced the Asia-based employees to stream the meetings late on Friday nights.

> "[At the Googleplex] I saw everything from a full-sized T-Rex skeleton replica to vegetable gardens to a volleyball court. In each building, Google seems to promote fitness and your overall well-being."[44]
>
> —Journalist Lance Ulanoff.

## Atmosphere of Creativity

There is no question that this atmosphere of creativity has been beneficial not only for Brin and Page—both have amassed personal fortunes in the billions of dollars—but also for their company and the billions of people who rely on Google to provide them with the information they need to help them navigate the Internet. In addition to AdSense and Gmail, other projects that have emerged from the Googleplex are Google Maps, which helps travelers plan their routes by giving them directions, route options, and estimates on travel time; and Google Translate, which enables users to enter sentences in one language and receive instant translations in other languages. By 2015 Google Translate enabled users to translate sentences into eighty-eight languages from Afrikaans to Zulu.

People who download the free Google Earth application for their computers or other devices can take virtual tours of many cities and rural areas—any place that has been photographed and uploaded into the Google Earth database. People searching for places to live can examine prospective neighborhoods, travelers can check out foreign cities they may want to visit, and students can find street-level views of some of the world's most important landmarks.

Google Chrome is Google's own web browser. According to the web tracking site Shareaholic, by 2013 some 35 percent of Internet users were relying on Chrome—making it the most popular browser. The speed of

The navigational tool Google Maps is just one of the many well-known and well-used products developed by the company. These and other Google innovations have made Brin and Page very wealthy.

## Google: The World's Most Attractive Employer

Since 2009 Google has been named the World's Most Attractive Employer by Universum, an international talent recruiting firm. To determine which employers are considered the most sought after by college students, Universum polls more than two hundred thousand business and engineering students.

According to the 2014 poll, students hope to land jobs with companies that offer creative work environments. Moreover, students do not want to feel as though they are being bossed around. Universum found both these qualities are prevalent at Google. "A friendly work environment is an indication that this generation, no matter wherever they are in the world, take a different approach to work," says Universum chief executive officer Petter Nylander. "Students know what a large role work will play in their lives and want to work in an environment that resonates—employers need to invest in cultivating this."

Since Google has ranked at the top of Universum's annual list since 2009, students clearly believe jobs at Google will be challenging but also fun. Students approaching graduation should know, however, that Google accepts the most accomplished engineering and business students only. In a typical year, Google hires between one thousand and four thousand employees—and it receives more than 1 million applicants for those jobs.

Quoted in Kathryn Dill, "The World's Most Attractive Employers 2014," *Forbes*, September 24, 2014. www.forbes.com.

the browser was cited as the primary reason for its popularity. In comparison, other browsers included Firefox, which found favor among 16.6 percent of Internet users; Safari, which recorded 16.2 percent of Internet users; and Internet Explorer, 15.6 percent. And as a companion to Chrome, Google partnered with hardware manufacturers to develop the Chromebook computer, a laptop that employs software stored in a central Google database—a sharp departure from how personal computers have been manufactured since the 1970s, in which all software is contained in each individual computer's hard drive. In other words, to use the Chromebook for most applications, the device must constantly be connected to the Internet.

## Challenges to Google

All of those projects and others are dedicated to the original mission statement: "To organize the world's information and make it universally accessible and useful."[47] But other projects developed under that declaration have not worked out as planned because, as Brin and Page have learned, organizing the world's information and making it accessible can sometimes violate people's rights.

The Google Books project serves as an example. In 2004 Brin and Page announced an ambitious undertaking to scan the pages of some 15 million books, making them available to be read online. Eventually, Brin and Page hoped to include 50 million books in the database—virtually every book in print. But Brin and Page soon encountered hostility from authors and publishers who held copyrights to published books. Copyrights ensure that authors and publishers maintain ownership of what they write and publish, thereby guaranteeing that they collect income from their books in the form of royalties. Royalties are paid whenever a customer purchases a print copy or downloads the e-book version of a work.

In 2005 two trade groups—the Authors Guild and the American Association of Publishers—sued Google, contending that copyright holders would be robbed of their royalty payments should their books be available for free through Google Books. Numerous other trade groups as well as individual authors filed their own lawsuits, tangling up the Google Books project in extensive litigation. By 2015 Brin and Page had resolved their differences with many of the parties that had sued them—often by paying them substantial fees—but some cases remained outstanding as of 2015.

For Internet users, though, the major impact of the legal challenges to Google Books has been the decision by Brin and Page to scale back the project. Books are still scanned, but most books that appear on Google Books include just a handful of pages. By including just some pages from the books, Google is able to abide by copyright laws that permit the "fair use" of a limited amount of material published in copyrighted works. Un-

The Google Books project began as an ambitious effort to scan and make available online virtually every book in print—about 50 million books. As a result of legal challenges, the company's cofounders scaled back their project.

der law, reprinting just a handful of pages from a book, or quoting from that book in another publication—whether it is print or online—does not violate the rights held by authors and publishers.

## Right to Be Forgotten

Yet another controversy could conceivably pose the greatest threat to Google's mission to organize the world's information. In 2014 the Court of Justice of the European Union, which presides over cases that affect most countries in Europe, ruled that people have the right to be excluded from Google searches. The court held that people should have the right to have embarrassing information in their pasts erased from the Internet. The courts called this the "right to be forgotten."[48]

The case was brought by Mario Costeja González, a Spaniard who insisted that Google searches turned up information about his formerly poor credit record—which he has since repaired. Therefore, he contended, Internet users should not have access to facts that are no longer relevant to his character or financial status.

Privacy advocates believe the ruling would be embraced by young people who post embarrassing pictures of themselves on social media sites, which they may later regret if prospective employers see the photos and deny them jobs based on conduct that is no longer reflective of their characters. Michael Fertik, chief executive of Reputation.com, which helps people remove embarrassing information about themselves from the Internet, insists, "For the first time, human dignity will get the same treatment online as copyright. It will be protected under the law. That's a huge deal."[49]

> "[Because of the 2014 Court of Justice of the European Union ruling], human dignity will get the same treatment online as copyright. It will be protected under the law. That's a huge deal."[49]
>
> —Michael Fertik, chief executive of Reputation.com.

Google had actually been voluntarily removing information about people from Google searches since 2008—always at the request of individuals. In 2014, due to the European court ruling, Google ramped up its efforts, complying with 345 million requests to remove information from its Internet searches—about double the number it received the previous year.

In response to the court's ruling, Page said he believes that access to information is a fundamental building block of free societies, and he feared that dictatorial governments would use the European court's decision as an excuse to cut off people's access to information that could possibly be used to expose repressive measures. He said, "It will be used by other governments that aren't as forward and progressive as Europe to do bad things. . . . Certainly, I worry about the effect that might have on democracy over time."[50]

## Challenging Modern Culture

The controversies over the European court ruling as well as Google Books illustrate that the mission formulated by Brin and Page—to organize and make accessible the world's information—does not always fit neatly into modern culture. Nevertheless, there is no question that the culture they created for their own company—which includes the 20 percent time rule and the unique work environment at the Googleplex—has produced ideas that often challenge the rules of modern society. Indeed, individuals like González would never have insisted they have the right to be forgotten unless Brin and Page used the culture of their company to make huge volumes of information available to anyone with access to the Internet.

# Chapter 5

# Taking Google into the Future

Except for the weekly TGIF conferences, Page and Brin are not believed to spend much time at the Googleplex. Instead, most of their time is reportedly spent at a secret office campus in Northern California known as Google X. Neither Page nor Brin—or any other Google executives—admit to the existence of Google X or openly discuss the projects under development at the secret lab. However, some news has leaked out.

In 2011 the *New York Times* reported on some of the innovations under study at Google X: "It's a place where your refrigerator could be connected to the Internet, so it could order groceries when they ran low. Your dinner plate could post to a social network what you're eating. Your robot could go to the office while you stay home in your pajamas. And you could, perhaps, take an elevator to outer space."[51] When questioned by reporters, Brin said only, "Where I spend my time is farther afield projects, which we hope will graduate to important key businesses in the future."[52]

> "Where I spend my time is farther afield projects, which we hope will graduate to important key businesses in the future."[52]
>
> —Google cocreator Sergey Brin.

The existence of Google X illustrates that Brin and Page are not content with maintaining Google as a company that collects income from web-based advertising—or even staying within their original mission to organize and make accessible the world's information. The two entrepreneurs are very interested in pursuing new technology they hope will revolutionize world society. "Periodically ... you should work on something new that you think is really amazing," says Page. "The trick is coming up with those products. . . . I think we need to be doing breakthrough, non-incremental things across our whole business."[53]

## Driverless Cars

Although they are hesitant to discuss projects under way at Google X, Brin and Page have been very public about the prospects for one of Google's most dynamic projects: Development of the driverless car. About one hundred prototypes have been built, and by early 2015 Google was actively testing them at a closed track. By then the cars had collectively logged some 700,000 miles (1.1 million km) on the test track, prompting Google to predict they would be ready for consumers by 2018. "This car can do 75 mph," says Chris Urmson, director of the project for Google. "It can track pedestrians and cyclists. It understands traffic lights. It can merge at highway speeds."[54]

*Brin and Page have high hopes for their self-driving car, pictured during a driving demonstration in the Googleplex parking lot in 2014. The driverless car idea is also being pursued by carmakers including BMW, Mercedes, and Tesla.*

The all-electric vehicles have been designed without steering wheels, brakes, or accelerator pedals and are instead equipped with sensors and software that help them maneuver through traffic. The passenger would have access to a control button that stops the car in the event of an emergency. Moreover, people may be able to summon the cars by employing an Internet-powered Global Positioning System technology that Google is testing. Says Brin, "We took a look from the ground up of what a self-driving car would look like."[55]

Brin and Page may have decided to talk about their driverless car program because Google is facing competition. Several automakers, including BMW, Mercedes, and Tesla, are also actively pursuing driverless cars. Therefore, Google finds itself in a race against competitors to introduce its driverless cars to the market.

According to Brin, the purpose of the driverless car is to revolutionize transportation—to provide mobility to people who are otherwise unable to drive. "What I'm excited about is how we could change transportation today," says Brin. "If you look at people who are too old, too young, or disabled, and can't get around, that's a big challenge for them."[56]

## Experimenting with Robots

Driverless cars are essentially robots—machines that can be programmed to perform physical tasks. In fact, robotics is a major area of study at Google X. Uses of robots under study at Google X range from employing them for simple household tasks, such as vacuuming the carpets, to using them outside the home to enhance Google's presence on the Internet. Reportedly, Page and Brin are interested in deploying robots to photograph every corner of the world so that there would be no gaps in the information people seek on Google Earth or through Google Maps.

Brin has long been interested in robotics and in 2010 made a very public demonstration of his interest when the BrinBot made its debut at a Silicon Valley robotics conference. About forty engineers and executives attended the conference—including Brin, except he was not physically in the room. Brin was represented by his robot, the BrinBot.

The BrinBot moved around the room on wheels attached to a heavy base, occasionally interacting with the human attendees. A head-high

## Google in Space

Larry Page and Sergey Brin have long been interested in pursuing space exploration. In 2014 Google paid $1.6 billion to NASA for a sixty-year lease on a NASA airfield near San Francisco. The facility includes three huge hangars capable of housing space exploration vehicles, which Google hopes to develop. Says Brin, "I am a big believer in the exploration and commercial development of the space frontier and am looking forward to the possibility of going into space."

One project that Google explored is the development of a space elevator. Since the 1960s countries have sent astronauts into space aboard rocket-propelled vehicles. Under the concept of a space elevator, a cable hundreds or even thousands of miles in length would be anchored to a station on the ground. The other end of the cable is attached to a satellite. A vehicle then rides up and down the cable, transporting astronauts to the satellite. "It could take you from ground to orbit with a net of basically zero energy," says Rich DeVaul, who headed the space elevator project for Google. "It drives down the space-access costs, operationally, to being incredibly low."

Although the space elevator was studied at Google X, engineers concluded that given the materials currently available to manufacture the cable, no substance exists that would make the cable strong enough to withstand the tremendous pressure of holding on to an orbiting satellite. The project has been shelved for the time being.

Quoted in Ned Potter, "Google Search: Sergey Brin Space Flight," ABC News, June 11, 2008. http://abc news.go.com.

Quoted in Jon Gertner, "The Truth About Google X: An Exclusive Look Behind the Secretive Lab's Closed Doors," *Fast Company*, April 15, 2014. www.fastcompany.com.

computer screen was attached to the top of the base, displaying a real-time stream of Brin's face as he controlled the robot and participated in the conference from his office in Mountain View. "I do think that a lot of the things that people do have been, over the past century, replaced by machines and will continue to be,"[57] says Brin. Page believes robots will help free people from mundane tasks, which will allow them to perform more meaningful work as well as enable them to make more use of their time for leisure. "Most people like working, but they'd also like to have more time with their family or to pursue their own interests,"[58] says Page.

The BrinBot made its debut at a conference sponsored by Singularity University, a Silicon Valley institution that provides graduate-level courses to engineers and scientists pursuing research in high-tech fields. Page founded Singularity University, providing $250,000 in personal funds to establish the school. Several other top Google executives have also contributed hundreds of thousands of dollars each.

## Project Ara

Driverless cars and robotics may be the most well-known innovations under way at Google, but as the *New York Times* story reported, there are many others. A refrigerator that can detect when the milk is low and responds by using the Internet to order a new carton from the supermarket is one way in which Google hopes to incorporate the Internet into operation of the household. One of Google's most successful ventures has been Android, an operating system for smartphones and similar devices. Android applications to link smartphones to all manner of household uses are under development as part of Google's Internet of Things project. Already, for example, people whose smartphones are powered by Android are able to turn the lights on and off at home or turn on the coffeepot so a fresh cup of coffee is ready by the time they get home. Google hopes to extend Android applications to many more household uses.

Google even hopes to reinvent the smartphone. At Google X, engineers are studying Project Ara, a new type of smartphone that users will be able to take apart themselves, adding or subtracting hardware as they need it. For example, if the user is a diabetes patient and he or she owns an Ara smartphone, the patient would be able to obtain a blood glucose monitoring module that plugs into the smartphone—a feature that many other smartphone users would not need. Or perhaps the Ara smartphone would have a removable module that provides it with photographic capability. If a better photographic module is developed, the user would not have to replace the whole smartphone to improve the camera, just the photography module.

Page and Brin are said to be closely following the development of Ara. *Fortune* magazine reported:

> [Their] army of Googlers is always searching for the next thing that will push the arc of technology forward. The result is a company unlike any other: always impatient, always moving and always searching for the next big thing. And that, of course, is what Page and Brin meant when they opened [a] letter to shareholders with these two sentences: "We are not a conventional company. We do not intend to become one."[59]

## Attacking Google Glass

Not all projects developed by Google have been going as smoothly as driverless cars or Project Ara. The development of Google Glass, for example, has featured more than a few stumbles.

Google Glass is a device people can employ as eyewear—similar to how they might wear prescription lenses. The user relays the commands to Google Glass by voice. As the user focuses his or her eyes on an object, a tiny projector imbedded in the lens beams information about the object directly onto the user's retina. For example, if the user visits the Washington Monument and wants to know more about the national landmark, the user may ask Google Glass to obtain information from the Internet about the monument: who designed the edifice, when it was erected, and so on.

According to Brin, Google Glass enables people to stay connected to the Internet without the need to be constantly looking down at their smartphones. Demonstrating Google Glass before an audience of engineers in 2013, Brin showed how the device performs many of the same

"[Google's] army of Googlers is always searching for the next thing that will push the arc of technology forward. The result is a company unlike any other: always impatient, always moving and always searching for the next big thing."[59]

—*Fortune* magazine.

functions as a smartphone but without the need for the user to be constantly staring at a handheld apparatus. He says:

> This position that you just saw me in, looking down at my phone, that's one of the reasons behind this project. . . . Because we ultimately questioned whether this is the ultimate future of how you want to connect to other people in your life, how you want to connect to information. Should it be by just walking around looking down? . . . In addition to potentially socially isolating yourself when you're out and about looking at your phone . . . is this what you're meant to do with your body? You're standing around there and you're just rubbing this featureless piece of glass.[60]

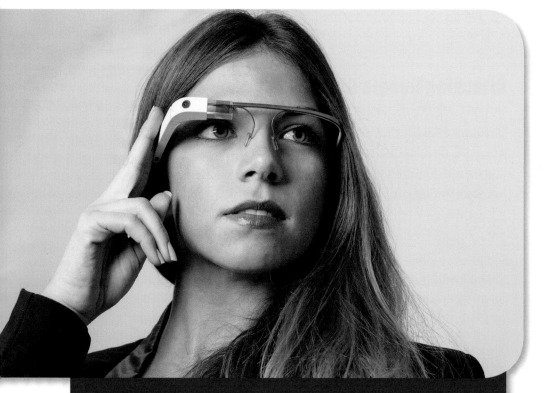

*The Google Glass Internet-connected eyewear won some early praise but also received a lot of criticism. The company considers it to be an experimental and long-term project.*

But Google Glass has raised criticism. Jay Yarow, a technology writer for the website Business Insider, had this to say about Google Glass: "I don't see a killer application that makes [Google Glass] worth it. . . . I just see a product plagued by bugs, of questionable use, that's generating a lot of buzz because people want so desperately to have some new gadget to latch onto, and fear being wrong about the next major technology trend."[61]

Among the deficiencies highlighted by Yarow were low battery life for the device, difficulty in reading the screen, and the headaches and other problems suffered by users who tested the eyewear. "It's disorientating," said Business Insider writer Alyson Shontell, who tested Google Glass. "You're unable to focus on people or things around you.... Glass is headache-inducing, too; you're more or less cross-eyed when focusing on something so close to your face."[62]

> "[Google Glass is] disorientating. You're unable to focus on people or things around you. . . . Glass is headache-inducing, too; you're more or less cross-eyed when focusing on something so close to your face."[62]
>
> —Alyson Shontell, a writer for Business Insider.

## Privacy Concerns

Headaches, low battery life, and a screen that is difficult to read are not the only issues that have been raised by critics of Google Glass. In giving Google Glass the same features as a smartphone, the developers have enabled people to use the device to take photos and videos as well as record audio—and post it all on social media if they desire. The difference between using a smartphone to snap a picture and Google Glass to take a photo is that when somebody uses a smartphone to record an image, they must point the smartphone at the subject. In other words, the person being photographed usually knows that he or she will be in the photo.

But Google Glass gives the wearer the capability of surreptitiously taking the photo—and posting the image on social media without the person in the photo knowing a photo has been taken or that the photo has been uploaded to a social media site. This has raised charges that Google Glass can be used as a tool to violate people's privacy. Says

## Smart Thermostats

Making the Internet into a more active component in the home was the idea that propelled Google Nest—a smart thermostat for home use. Programmable thermostats are not new; for many years homeowners have been able to program their thermostats to reduce the heat when they are away from home or at night when they are asleep. Google Nest takes thermostats a step further.

Electric companies respond to demand—on very hot days, for example, they have to produce a lot more electricity because a lot of people turn up their air-conditioning. During such peak demand periods, the price for electricity will rise. Nest responds to these peak demand periods by reducing the electricity supplied to nonessential gadgets in the home. Nest may, for example, delay a clothes dryer cycle until demand—and therefore the price of the electricity—is reduced.

Electric companies have to agree to let Google link Nest systems to their operating systems; by 2015 some companies had provided Google with the links. Clearly, electric companies see systems like Nest becoming very common in American homes. Says personal finance journalist Travis Hoium, "If a utility in your area participates in the program you could save money by simply signing up and allowing Google to automatically turn down your load when your utility wants you to. This could turn into a big business for Google."

Travis Hoium, "Why Google's Future Growth Is in Energy," Motley Fool, January 10, 2015. www.fool.com.

Charles Arthur, a technology writer for the *Guardian*, a British newspaper, "People are already beginning to fret about the social implications of Glass. . . . The first, and most obvious, is the question of privacy. The second is: How will we behave in groups when the distraction of the Internet is only an eye movement away?"[63]

Another journalist, Joshua Topolsky, pointed out that he wore a test version of Google Glass while attempting to film a story at a coffee shop. He entered the shop with a film crew and was asked by the manager not to film in the restaurant because cameras violated the privacy of the patrons. Topolsky agreed to stop filming but kept wearing his Google Glass, giving him the ability to keep filming without the coffee shop owner or patrons knowing. "I kept the Glass's video recording going, all the way through,"[64] says Topolsky. This gave him the power to secretly violate the restriction and led him to worry about the potential uses of such surreptitious recording devices.

Brin and Page have responded to their critics. They insist the hardware issues that have been uncovered in the early Google Glass tests will be resolved. As for the privacy issues, in a statement issued in 2014 the company said, "If a company sought to design a secret spy device, they could do a better job than Glass! Let's be honest: if someone wants to secretly record you, there are much, much better cameras out there than one you wear conspicuously on your face and that lights up every time you give a voice command, or press a button."[65] Nevertheless, by early 2015 Google Glass was still considered an experimental product. Google had not yet made plans to mass-produce the wearable device.

## Google.org

If Google Glass is ultimately released as a product for consumers, the device will undoubtedly add to the enormous profits the company has enjoyed over the years. And although Google has fulfilled the intentions of Brin and Page to be a profitable venture, the two founders have created a nonprofit arm of the company, Google.org, which uses Google's resources to find ways to improve people's lives without concerns about returning profits to the company.

Among the projects under development by Google's nonprofit division are new ways to collect solar energy as well as map sources of geothermal energy—sources of heat that lie below the surface of the earth. This heat can be tapped to warm homes without creating carbon-based pollution. Another project that focuses on an anti-pollution measure is development of a new engine for a hybrid car that runs on electricity and ethanol. Currently, hybrid cars are powered by electric motors and internal combustion engines powered by gasoline. Ethanol would be less polluting than gasoline because it is a form of alcohol distilled from vegetables. "We're not doing it for the profit," says Larry Brilliant, a physician

In addition to creating a highly profitable company, Google cofounders Sergey Brin (left) and Larry Page (right) have established a nonprofit arm that is working on various projects. Among these are efforts to develop new ways of providing and using renewable energy.

appointed by Brin and Page as director of Google.org. "And if we didn't get our capital back, so what? The emphasis is on social returns, not economic returns."[66]

## New Paths in Technology

The establishment of Google.org illustrates that Page and Brin are no longer concerned that they will suffer the same fate as Nikola Tesla. They have certainly profited from PageRank, AdWords, AdSense, and all the other ways Google has revolutionized Internet search and commerce. Now they seem more concerned about using the tremendous resources of their company to improve life on the planet. No longer content with just managing the world's information and making it accessible to all, Brin and Page are forging new paths in technology, making the achievements of the world's top engineers and scientists accessible to all.

## Introduction: Managing the World's Information

1. Quoted in Candace Lombardi, "Google Joins Xerox as a Verb," CNET News, July 6, 2006. http://news.cnet.com.

2. Quoted in George Beahm, ed., *The Google Boys: Sergey Brin and Larry Page in Their Own Words*. Evanston, IL: Agate, 2014. Kindle edition.

3. Quoted in Google, "Google's Mission Is to Organize the World's Information and Make It Universally Accessible and Useful," April 14, 2014. www.google.com.

4. Quoted in Beahm, *The Google Boys*.

## Chapter One: Brin and Page: Their Paths to Stanford

5. Quoted in Ken Auletta, *Googled: The End of the World as We Know It*. New York: Penguin, 2009, pp. 28–29.

6. Quoted in David A. Vise and Mark Malseed, *The Google Story: Inside the Hottest Business, Media and Technology Success of Our Time*. New York: Bantam Dell, 2008, p. 26.

7. Quoted in Daniel Alef, *The Gatekeepers: Sergey Brin, Larry Page and Google*. Santa Barbara, CA: Titans of Fortune, 2011. Kindle edition.

8. Quoted in Auletta, *Googled*, p. 29.

9. Quoted in Mark Malseed, "The Story of Sergey Brin," *Moment*, February/March 2007. www.momentmag.com.

10. Quoted in Malseed, "The Story of Sergey Brin."

11. Quoted in Vise and Malseed, *The Google Story*, pp. 23–24.

12. Quoted in Auletta, *Googled*, p. 33.

13. Quoted in Auletta, *Googled*, p. 33.

14. Quoted in Auletta, *Googled*, p. 33.

15. Quoted in Auletta, *Googled*, p. 34.

16. Quoted in Vise and Malseed, *The Google Story*, p. 25.

17. Quoted in John Battelle, "The Birth of Google," *Wired*, August 2005. http://archive.wired.com.

18. Quoted in Battelle, "The Birth of Google."

## Chapter Two: How Brin and Page Revolutionized Internet Searching

19. Alexander Halavais, *Search Engine Society*. Cambridge: Polity, 2009. Kindle edition.

20. Al Gore, "Remarks Prepared for Delivery by Vice President Al Gore," University of California–Los Angeles, January 11, 1994. www.ibiblio .org.

21. Quoted in Battelle, "The Birth of Google."

22. Quoted in Battelle, "The Birth of Google."

23. Auletta, *Googled*, p. 39.

24. Quoted in Vise and Malseed, *The Google Story*, p. 39.

25. Quoted in Vise and Malseed, *The Google Story*, p. 39.

## Chapter Three: Turning Google into Big Business

26. Quoted in John Battelle, *The Search: How Google and Its Rivals Rewrote the Rules of Business and Transformed Our Culture*. New York: Penguin, 2005, p. 85.

27. Quoted in Battelle, *The Search*, pp. 81–82.

28. Quoted in Battelle, *The Search*, p. 87.

29. Quoted in Auletta, *Googled*, p. 45.

30. *PC Magazine*, "Google," Wayback Machine, 1998. http://web.archive .org.

31. Quoted in Vise and Malseed, *The Google Story*, p. 59.

32. Quoted in Auletta, *Googled*, p. 44.

33. Quoted in Auletta, *Googled*, p. 44.

34. Sergey Brin and Lawrence Page, "The Anatomy of a Large-Scale Hypertextual Web Search Engine," Stanford University, 1998. http://info lab.stanford.edu.

35. Brin and Page, "The Anatomy of a Large-Scale Hypertextual Web Search Engine."

36. Ken Auletta, *Googled*, pp. 52–53.

37. Quoted in Will Oremus, "Google's Big Break," *Slate*, October 13, 2013. www.slate.com.

38. Quoted in Beahm, *The Google Boys*.

39. Oremus, "Google's Big Break."

## Chapter Four: Creating a Culture of Creativity

40. Quoted in Laura He, "Google's Secrets of Innovation: Empowering Its Employees," *Forbes*, March 29, 2013. www.forbes.com.

41. Quoted in Auletta, *Googled*, p. 91.

42. Quoted in Beahm, *The Google Boys*.

43. Vise and Malseed, *The Google Story*, pp. 152–153.

44. Lance Ulanoff, "The Googleplex: Everything You've Heard Is True," *PC Magazine*, March 28, 2009. www.pcmag.com.

45. Ulanoff, "The Googleplex."

46. Quoted in Beahm, *The Google Boys*.

47. Quoted in Google, "Google's Mission Is to Organize the World's Information and Make It Universally Accessible and Useful."

48. Quoted in Alan Travis and Charles Arthur, "EU Court Backs 'Right to Be Forgotten': Google Must Amend Results on Request," *Guardian* (London), May 13, 2014. www.theguardian.com.

49. Quoted in David Streitfeld, "European Court Lets Users Erase Records on Web," *New York Times*, May 14, 2014, p. A1.

50. Quoted in Samuel Gibbs, "Larry Page: 'Right to Be Forgotten' Could Empower Government Repression," *Guardian* (London), May 30, 2014. www.theguardian.com.

## Chapter Five: Taking Google into the Future

51. Claire Cain Miller and Nick Bilton, "Google's Lab of Wildest Dreams," *New York Times*, November 14, 2011, p. A1.

52. Quoted in Miller and Bilton, "Google's Lab of Wildest Dreams," p. A1.

53. Quoted in Steven Levy, "Google's Larry Page on Why Moon Shots Matter," *Wired*, January 17, 2013. www.wired.com.

54. Quoted in Tom Vanderbilt, "Let the Robot Drive: The Autonomous Car of the Future Is Here," *Wired*, January 20, 2012. www.wired.com.

55. Quoted in Jessica Guynn, "Google Rolling Out Its Own Driverless Car," *USA Today*, May 28, 2014. www.usatoday.com.

56. Quoted in Guynn, "Google Rolling Out Its Own Driverless Car."

57. Quoted in Samuel Gibbs, "Google's Founders on the Future of Health, Transport—and Robots," *Guardian* (London), July 7, 2014. www.theguardian.com.

58. Quoted in Gibbs, "Google's Founders on the Future of Health, Transport—and Robots."

59. Quoted in Miguel Helft, "Google: Still an Unconventional Company," *Fortune*, August 19, 2014. http://fortune.com.

60. Quoted in Joseph Geni and Morton Bast, "Sergey Brin: Why Google Glass?," transcript, TED, February 2013. www.ted.com.

61. Jay Yarow, "The Verdict Is In: Nobody Likes Google Glass," Business Insider, May 3, 2013. www.businessinsider.com.

62. Quoted in Yarow, "The Verdict Is In."

63. Charles Arthur, "Google Glass: Is It a Threat to Our Privacy?," *Guardian* (London), March 6, 2013. www.theguardian.com.

64. Quoted in Arthur, "Google Glass."

65. Quoted in Stuart Dredge, "Google Hits Back at the Google Glass Haters in 'Top 10 Myths' Blog Post," *Guardian* (London), March 20, 2014. www.theguardian.com.

66. Quoted in Katie Hafner, "Philanthropy Google's Way: Not the Usual," *New York Times*, September 14, 2006. www.nytimes.com.

# Important Events in the Lives of Sergey Brin and Larry Page

## 1969
Computers at Stanford University and the University of California, Los Angeles exchange information over telephone lines, establishing the Internet.

## 1973
Larry Page is born on March 26; Sergey Brin is born on August 21.

## 1979
The Brin family gains permission to leave the Soviet Union; in October the Brins arrive in America.

## 1990
Brin graduates from Eleanor Roosevelt High School in Baltimore, Maryland, and enters the University of Maryland. In Canada, engineering student Alan Emtage develops Archie, the first Internet search engine.

## 1991
Page graduates from East Lansing High School in Michigan and enters the University of Michigan.

## 1993
Brin graduates from the University of Maryland and enters the graduate computer science program of Stanford University.

## 1994
Congress mandates that telecommunications companies provide unrestricted access to the Internet.

## 1995
Page graduates from the University of Michigan and enters Stanford, where he meets Brin.

## 1996
Brin and Page begin work on PageRank, an algorithm to rank websites based on their links, and BackRub, a search engine.

## 1997
Page and Brin change the name of BackRub to Google, and on September 15 Page registers the domain name.

## 1998
Page and Brin drop out of Stanford to build Google as a business.

## 2000
Google becomes the most popular search engine, used 30 million times a day; in October Brin and Page launch AdWords.

## 2001
Google turns its first profit, earning $7 million for its investors.

## 2004
Google's headquarters, the Googleplex, opens in Mountain View, California.

## 2006
Editors of *Merriam-Webster's Collegiate Dictionary* accept the verb *google* as a word for inclusion in the dictionary's next edition; Google acquires YouTube.

## 2014
A European court rules that people have the right to have information about them removed from Google searches.

## 2015
Wall Street values Google at more than $370 billion.

# For Further Research

## Books

George Beahm, ed., *The Google Boys: Sergey Brin and Larry Page in Their Own Words*. Evanston, IL: Agate, 2014. Kindle edition.

Walter Isaacson, *The Innovators: How a Group of Hackers, Geniuses, and Geeks Created the Digital Revolution*. New York: Simon & Schuster, 2014.

Donald A. Norman, *The Design of Everyday Things*. New York: Basic Books, 2013.

John J. O'Neill, *Prodigal Genius: The Life of Nikola Tesla*. New York: Cosimo, 2006.

Eric Schmidt and Jonathan Rosenberg, *How Google Works*. New York: Grand Central, 2014.

## Periodicals

Charles Arthur, "Google Glass: Is It a Threat to Our Privacy?," *Guardian* (London), March 6, 2013.

Jessica Guynn, "Google Rolling Out Its Own Driverless Car," *USA Today*, May 28, 2014.

Laura He, "Google's Secrets of Innovation: Empowering Its Employees," *Forbes*, March 29, 2013.

Miguel Helft, "Google: Still an Unconventional Company," *Fortune*, August 19, 2014.

Steven Levy, "Google's Larry Page on Why Moon Shots Matter," *Wired*, January 17, 2013.

Alan Travis and Charles Arthur, "EU Court Backs 'Right to Be Forgotten': Google Must Amend Results on Request," *Guardian* (London), May 13, 2014.

# Websites

**About Google** (www.google.com/about). Google maintains this site to provide news about the company as well as links to Google's philosophy on how it manages information available on the Internet. By following the link for Doodles, visitors can explore how Google occasionally changes its logo to reflect a national holiday, birthday of an important inventor or innovator, or similar anniversary of importance.

**"The Anatomy of a Large-Scale Hypertextual Web Search Engine"** (http://infolab.stanford.edu/~backrub/google.html). The 1998 paper written by Brin and Page explains PageRank. Despite the paper's technical nature and title, and its occasional reliance on mathematical formulas, PageRank is explained in easy-to-follow steps, illustrating how Brin and Page employed the wisdom of crowds approach in revolutionizing Internet search.

**Google.org** (www.google.org). Google's nonprofit arm maintains this website to provide information on the company's public service projects. By 2015 some of the projects that were being funded by Google.org were immunizing Africans to protect them against Ebola, empowering women and girls to pursue careers, and improving computer science education in American schools.

**Larry Page** (https://plus.google.com/+LarryPage/posts). Larry Page's page on Google+, Google's social networking site, is used by Page to provide links for issues he finds of interest, such as innovations in technology. He is also known to post comments about other matters—such as his mother's pancake recipe. He has more than 8.8 million followers.

**Sergey Brin's Home Page** (http://infolab.stanford.edu/~sergey). Sergey Brin's Stanford University home page is still alive on the Internet. Visitors can see a photo of Brin during his Stanford years, read about Brin's background, and access some of the scientific papers Brin wrote during his years as a student.

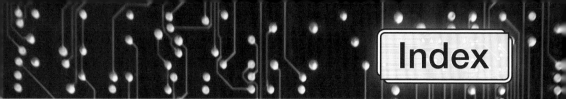

# Index

# Picture Credits

# About the Author

Hal Marcovitz is a former newspaper reporter and columnist. He has written more than 170 books for young readers. He makes his home in Chalfont, Pennsylvania.